44

CW00669980

REMEMBRANCE

AGATHA CHRISTIE

Illustrated by Richard Allen

SOUVENIR PRESS

IF I should leave you in the days
to come—

GOD grant that may not be—

BUT yet if so,

I died—but not my love for you,

THAT lives for aye—though dumb,

Remember this

I<small>F</small> I should leave you in the days
to come.

Y<small>OUR</small> love for me must fade I
know.

You will remember—and you will forget.

Bᴜᴛ oh! imperishable—strong

My love for you shall burn and glow

DEEP in your heart—your whole
life long,

UNKNOWN, unseen, but living
still in bliss

So you shall bear me with you
all the days.

ISBN 0 285 62876 3

Photoset and printed in Great Britain by
Redwood Burn Limited, Trowbridge, Wiltshire.

FORGET then what you will.